Steps Along The Way

LINDA LUCAS WALLING

Balboa Press books may be ordered through booksellers or by contacting:

Balboa Press
A Division of Hay House
1663 Liberty Drive
Bloomington, IN 47403
www.balboapress.com
1 (877) 407-4847

ISBN: 978-1-5043-4767-9 (sc)
ISBN: 978-1-5043-4768-6 (e)

Library of Congress Control Number: 2015921047

Print information available on the last page.

Balboa Press rev. date: 3/16/2016

BALBOA.
PRESS
A DIVISION OF HAY HOUSE

My Rhythms are unique to me.
I lumber and lurch along.
Broken rhythms set me apart.
I don't fit. I can't hide.
    CP destroys the illusion I could be perfect.
Balance and grace are lost to me –
Stiff, twisted, unsymmetrical.
Still photos can forgive.
Video never does.
    CP destroys the illusion I could be perfect.
I grasp and grip and drop without intent.
The brain (not mine) sends its unwanted cues.
    CP destroys the illusion I could be perfect.
"It takes two hands" I often say,
  asking for help with buttons, fasteners, snaps.
The tiny and delicate are easily destroyed in my hand.
    CP destroys the illusion I could be perfect.
Without it – what would I be?
A ballet dancer, light and graceful?
A sculptor chiseling wood or stone?
A seamstress skilled with thread and needle?
    CP destroys the illusion I could be perfect.
Without it – what would I be?
Still seeking perfection? Unwilling to seek help?
Unwilling to accept it?
Or would I be at all?
    CP destroys the illusion I could be perfect.

Introduction

Some people experience healing miracles and are suddenly transformed. Others, like me, set out on the path putting one foot after the other, sometimes finding a smooth highway, other times finding the path muddy and treacherous. I believe miracles can happen for any of us, and I welcome the time when I allow myself to experience mine. In the meantime, I take my steps and celebrate the way stations and landmarks as I reach them.

This series of poems is not about seeking and arriving at a final destination. Instead, the poems are about a segment of my journey during which I began to discover and trust the loving support and guidance that has always been available for me. It's available for all of us, of course. That was part of my discovery.

Each of us has our own journey influenced by many factors. From birth, we create our own interpretation of our lives on this earth. Our early interpretations become the foundation of our personal belief systems and – unless we change our stories or let go of them – they rule the rest of our lives for better or for worse. My own early interpretations established my beliefs that I was unworthy, unlovable, incapable, unprotected ...

I'll share just a bit of my journey to the point where I fell and became unable to walk in 2011. Spirit forcefully delivered the message that I had to change my story. I had not been paying attention to subtler warnings.

I was born in late 1939. It was the beginning of World War II in a time when society assumed that eugenics* (an early attempt at genetic engineering) was a worthy goal. The horror of the Holocaust was one outcome. Long after the Holocaust there was a widespread practice of sterilizing people who were considered to be "mentally defective" including people with mental illness, cognitive impairments, and an array of physical imperfections. Society feared that "the defectives" would pass on their "flaws" to future generations.

My mother told me that my birth was uneventful. When I was about six months old, I experienced a seizure after my second whooping cough shot.** The seizure caused relatively mild cerebral palsy affecting my left arm and leg. I have limited use of my left arm (which is two inches shorter than my right one). From childhood I walked with a limp, but I did walk. I experienced all of the teasing and cruelty that children with disabilities still experience today.

My parents were extremely overprotective. They, especially my mother, discouraged me from taking risks with physical activity because I "might get hurt." Early on, Mom decided that I would not be capable of life as a farm wife raising children. She focused on my education and my intellectual skills. I received the message loud and clear. I was unworthy of having a home and a family. The only useful thing about me was my brain.

It didn't help that I was born into a farm family in a lightly-populated area of rural Iowa. I grew up largely isolated from other children because there were so few farms near us where children my age lived. I attended one-room schools through the eighth grade with anywhere from six to twelve students at all grade levels. In the summer, I rarely saw other children except at Sunday School or Bible School. My social skills and self-confidence were poor. Mom encouraged me to join a 4-H club, but I quickly became ashamed of my inability to do the things other girls did with ease. I dropped out. When I began high school and encountered nearly a hundred students in my freshman class, I was overwhelmed. It wasn't until I was in college that I began to gradually heal, but I still perceived myself to be seriously flawed and unworthy of having anything beyond an intellectual life. I have actively fought that perception for many years, but remnants stay with me still today. It doesn't help that one of my core beliefs is that "nothing comes easy" – a phrase I heard often in my childhood from my Depression-era parents and grandparents.

Jumping fifty years ahead, by late 2011 I had become exhausted in mind, body and spirit. I spent nearly thirty years in an intense career as a university professor in South Carolina. While I was still teaching, my only brother died, and I gained responsibility for the care of my elderly parents who were some thousand miles away. Added to that, my husband's health, never good, was steadily deteriorating. (I had married at age fifty-one.) I was taking on more and more responsibility as his caregiver. Because of my core beliefs, I felt I had to do everything alone.

I retired from the university in 2003. That lightened my load, but the stress remained. By 2005 both of my parents had died, and that again eased the load. My focus became the increasing demands of my husband's situation, but I knew my body needed help. I began to study tai chi with a highly skilled sifu. My goal was to strengthen my bones. Tai chi was a major step for me. Throughout my life I had consistently avoided doing physical things. The diagnosis of osteoporosis and the fear of falling and breaking a hip overcame my dislike for physical activity. Tai chi was healing to my mind, body and spirit, and it provided me with a strong support system in my teacher and my classmates, but I did not tell any of them about the full weight of the load I carried.

Finally, in late 2011 my body had taken too much, and I fell on "my cerebral palsy side." My body tightened in the way it had after the seizure following the whooping cough shot. There were no broken bones, but I could not walk. There was no choice but to ask for help. My husband and I turned to the complimentary medicine community and my tai chi teacher. These friends kept me on my healing path. They have also helped me identify my other resources, especially my spiritual ones. (At the time of the fall, I was alienated from God, so I had to rediscover that support.)

Through these people I rediscovered my lifelong connection to Mother Mary. As far back as I can remember, I felt that God and Jesus had abandoned me. I grew up in a conservative evangelical church. I prayed as a child, but my child-self got no answer. Although I didn't realize it until recently, by the time I was three, Mother Mary (an anathema to evangelicals) had insinuated herself into my life. My church gave me no reason to feel that she had failed me, and I loved her and admired her. My parents' Catholic friends sent us Christmas cards each year with beautiful images of Mary. I shuffled through the cards with Christmas trees, Santas, snowflakes, and wrapped presents, to find my treasured cards—images of Mary. In the nearby town where we shopped there was a business that sold cemetery monuments. On outside display there was a beautiful tall gray granite monument with a figure of Mary. I always watched for her as we passed. I saw an ad for the movie Song of Bernadette when I was about five and campaigned to go and see it. My grandmother, surprisingly, agreed to take me, and I was entranced. For most of my life, though, Mary faded into the background. I know now that she stayed with me.

I began to reconnect with her in the late 1990s when I discovered an interest in the Great Mother. I was teaching a course titled Humanities Information Sources and Services. Mythology and religion were a part of that course. In updating my notes for the class one year, I browsed the bookshelves at a local bookstore. I discovered Lauren Artress' recently published book on Christian labyrinths. Because of my great interest in sacred symbols, I was fascinated. I was even more excited when I realized that Artress and her labrynths, based on the one at Chartres, were located at Grace Cathedral in San Francisco. San Francisco was the location of the next American Library Association annual conference. I would be attending. I made sure to find time to walk the labyrinth twice during that conference. At later ALA conferences held in that city, I walked the labyrinth.

In the early months after my fall, Mary began to appear in my dreams – a tall, large-boned, sturdy, late middle-aged woman who always wore a long dark blue cloak with a hood that hid her face. She had a solid, no-nonsense gait, and she wore sensible shoes. Her hands were large, work-worn and strong. In the dreams, she almost always held the hands of small children as she walked on the beach or sat in a lawn swing -- children snuggled against her or played nearby. Sometimes she held an infant cradled in one arm as she slowly rocked in the swing.

My friends helped me realize that she was a spiritual entity I could trust. She, and they, guided me to connect with my guardian angel and my spirit guides, some of whom I had known about before but hadn't contacted. My relationship with Jesus and The Source of All Things (which I prefer to call Great Spirit) improved, but there were many blocks. I still resisted asking for help from Great Spirit and the guides. I still thought I had to "do it all myself." I asked my friends for help when I had no other choice. To ask for help meant that I was lazy and babyish. I had improved in asking for human help, but I felt unworthy of spiritual help. I was aware of my guides. I didn't want to bother them or offend them. I rarely asked. That was where I found myself in 2013.

Journaling in an honest way has always been difficult for me. Instead of journaling, I turned to writing poetry and to colored pencil drawing. I had written poems and drawn before, but in 2013 the poems and drawings changed. I struggled to allow myself to ask for and accept help and guidance from the spiritual realm. The short poems that make up the body of this book were written in that year. I began with an image or insight from dreams or meditation. Sometimes a challenging issue was confronting me. I sat with the images or issue and allowed words to come and shape themselves. My drawing changed. I needed to allow myself to relax and let go, not draw for perfection. I drew some dream images using a doodling style. I asked Bridget, the playful guide who helps me be creative, to help me draw intuitively from my subconscious. The drawing and the poetry became meditations. I scribbled three or four overlapping lines of different colors intuitively. Then I asked for guidance from all my guides to see meaningful visual messages. I was amazed at what I discovered: animals, birds, flowers, hearts, trees, faces, traditional spiritual symbols. I colored the shapes of the images I saw and discovered that coloring revealed still more images. Books on dream images, animal totems and crystals helped me understand the messages in the drawings. Knowledgable advisors helped me understand the messages. Days and years later I go back to the drawings and see new messages.

Most of the illustrations that appear in this book are either dream images or doodled drawings. I continue to celebrate the way stations and landmarks as I reach them. I hope that reading about my journey and growth will lead people to allow themselves to create their own belief systems and to find the loving support and guidance that is always available.

The steps continue, of course, on into the future. That's the nature of The Way! They were halting steps in 2014 when my husband's situation deteriorated to the point where he was first hospitalized, then in rehabilitation for several months, and now in assisted living. Through that year, I found myself to again be physically and emotionally drained. Great Spirit, Mother Mary, Jesus, Archangel Michael, my guardian angel and my spirit guides – along with my human support – did not desert me. At the time of this writing, I have gained strength, confidence and trust. I am discovering ways to intuitively use my gifts. My body is stronger. The pain in my hip and knee is greatly diminished, and my tai chi standing practice has strengthened my leg and improved my balance. I am working with a physical therapist and am able to walk a few steps. With an adaptive walker, I hope to be much more independent. Taoist philosophy identifies Three Treasures (Mind, Body, and Spirit). To fully use one's gifts, the three must be in balance. The meditative poems, drawings, Tai Chi and Chi Gung represent important steps in my journey to heal my mind and spirit. Along with physical therapy, they are also important steps in healing my body. Gradually, the three come into balance. The challenge becomes to maintain the balance.

Spirit has led me to share these poems and drawings publicly. I trust that at least one reader will find words and images here that help on his or her path. My own journey to complete trust continues in faith. When I release the core belief that "nothing comes easy," I will set the stage for my miracle. LLW

————

*Eugenics: "The science of improving a human population by controlled breeding to increase the occurrence of desirable heritable characteristics."

**In the mid 1940s it was discovered that infants who had a reaction to the first whooping cough shot should not be given the second one. That bit of information was not known in 1940 when I received my second shot. (http://www.cdc.gov/vaccines/hcp/vis/vis-statements/dtap.html)

The Poems

I have chosen to leave the order of the poems written in 2013 unchanged. I have not edited out repetitions. Transitions from thrilling highs to depressing lows, and the occasional doubling back, reveal my jagged, non-linear path. My path is not smooth and straightforward. It is my hope that by following my wandering twists and turns, my double backs and leaps ahead, readers will accept their own less than linear journey.

The poem *My Rhythms* that precedes the introduction was written nearly twenty years ago. I recently rediscovered it. The issues I struggled with in 2013 may or may not have originated in my cerebral palsy, but CP certainly has had a strong influence on my life. The poems in the Prologue were also written a number of years ago and reflect some highs and lows in my life before 2013. The poem about the golden fleece was inspired by an exercise in the book Energy Vampires (see Resources). The poem in the Postscript was written in 1995 to accompany photographs of Judy Hubbard's exhibit of her magnificent time-themed paintings on gold-washed white silk curtains. Time is timeless. The journey is now.

I have included a few notes at the end of the book to explain obscure references.

Prologue

Beautiful Light slips through the cracks,
seeking a place to play.
Still dust in the closed-off mow holds her firm in place,
stagnating, stifling joy.

Sounds below--a ladder slides in place,
the trap pops open with a burst of air.
Dust darts up and down,
spiraling all around.

Beautiful Light leaps and sings.
Rainbow colors climb and fall,
twinkling, sparkling,
laughing in the swirling air.

I am here, pressed flat.
No color, not even black and white.
Just gray.

The Steps...

Sheltered by the strength that's gone before,
new life in its cozy nest –
all possibilities there in one.

I flow with the wind,
        kissing the trees.
                All nature smiles.

            Frozen auric layers,
        a nest to shelter Brave Heart
in this earthly moment.

           That first particle, Mother-Father to us all.
     We sibling rivals fight to separate,
                  bound together
        by our oneness.

From Emptiness, a tiny spark explodes.
Life and death begin – orchestrated chaos.
                    Love flows over all.

        I am touched by love in all my cells.
        I am surrounded, embedded in Love.
            I am a sponge, absorbing all.
            I am a crystal, refracting all.

        My heart soars, seeking the Oneness.
                Catching glimpses – glimpses only.
                Oh, the feast of Oneness!

        And so it goes – one step at a time.
    Learn to listen, learn to trust that I'll be led
                through debris and fog to
that place where I must be.

Somewhere deep within, a tiny voice longs
          to swell and sing with joy.

          Can you see me among myriad flashes of light?
               Can I see you?
        Flashing sparks of Love – all one Light.

How do I find my way?
Trust in unending, unconditional Love.
TRUST!
Allow healing Love to flow.
ALLOW!
Yield to the Love that flows
      softly and gently, washing away
           fear and distrust.
Accept the caresses.

      Rage transformed by Love.
Warm and giving, opening out
           Joining.
Nourishing within, without.

Rage turned inward.
Burning acid, corroding,
sealing off,
isolating.
Eating away all within.

No borders or boundaries,
    no defenses – open to everything.
  Flying apart into forever. No
grounding.

Ah, but I feel the angels surrounding me
softly stroking, gently supporting.
Here's the grounding.
It's true. Separate, I'm inadequate.
In the Oneness – total support.

Angels surround me, softly stroking, gentle support.
I'm grounded in the Love.

                    Brave Heart pierces the illusion,
                needs no nest, no safe place.
            At rest in undulating Stillness.

Who needs boundaries and defenses?
        My soul is grounded in the Love.
    No Illusion—only Love.

                Boundaries are illusion.
        Only ceaseless flow –
                    yin to yang, yang to yin.

I am pure love. My soul, my spirit, body, mind.
                My human self created by the Universe.
        For this brief second, stabilized
                in an illusion of separation.
                        Still, pure Love!

One tiny point in "time,"
       undulating, stable for this instant.
     Coiling, connecting, never stable.
   No points in timelessness.
       Only my center, my flowing perspective.

In forgiving myself I forgive all beings.
I forgive the Universe.
The Universe needs no forgiveness – only to be.
No need, no need.
I need no forgiveness – only to be.

Ceaseless flow:
yin to yang,
yang to yin.
Boundaries are illusion. Joy is in the flow.

One step at a time. Listen, trust that I'll be led
through debris and fog
to boundless, endless Spirit Love.

Unconditional Love crushes?
          No, it opens but does not shatter.

The Universe is empty of all but relationships.

My spirit flows free
          unencumbered by needs, fears,
              grief and regret.
          Free to love in pure perfection.

Great Spirit leads through the darkness to the Light.

My broken, frightened spirit cautiously allows
release from
        separation, stoicism and control.
    Opens to the One, trusts, allows dependence.

My magnificent self, boundless and exuberant, runs free
Through the Universe.
The Universe laughs with joy!

Great Spirit, Loving Spirit gently nudges Beautiful Pure Light:
"Open to Brave Heart and trust!"

Beautiful Pure Light, perfect and loving,
embraces joy,
opens to adventure.

Beautiful Pure Light seeks to flow unimpeded.
Brave Heart, on alert, ready —
awaiting fear and need's dissolving.

Heaven's lightning strikes.
Light's power flows,
cleansing all in its advance.

Flashes on the water, on the stones.
Flashes in the sky, spiraling through me.
I refract light to all the Universe.

23

A flash from above penetrates me, cuts through
                          all the blocks—
    Direct to the core of my being.
    Grounds me, lifts me, blesses me.
                    I stand tall, open, ready.

To be one with the Oneness – the fullness of belonging.
                    That's where I belong.

                        I long to cry. I fear to cry.
                    It's dangerous. Uncontrolled.
            How can I protect myself? I can't.
        Still,
            Love caresses anger, fear and hate.
                        Compassion cradles sadness.
    Beautiful Pure Light opens to the Love –
                only Love's protection for the journey.
                        I am one with Love.

The strength of water, the strength of rain,
                the strength of tears,
    washes away all debris that blocks the flow.

      Healing tears come when it's time,
              when they're allowed.
   No effort, no demands –
         only relaxation and openness.

Stillness leads me – awash in Love.
   No destination -- only deep knowing and trust to
       recline in the current –
        only the current of Love.

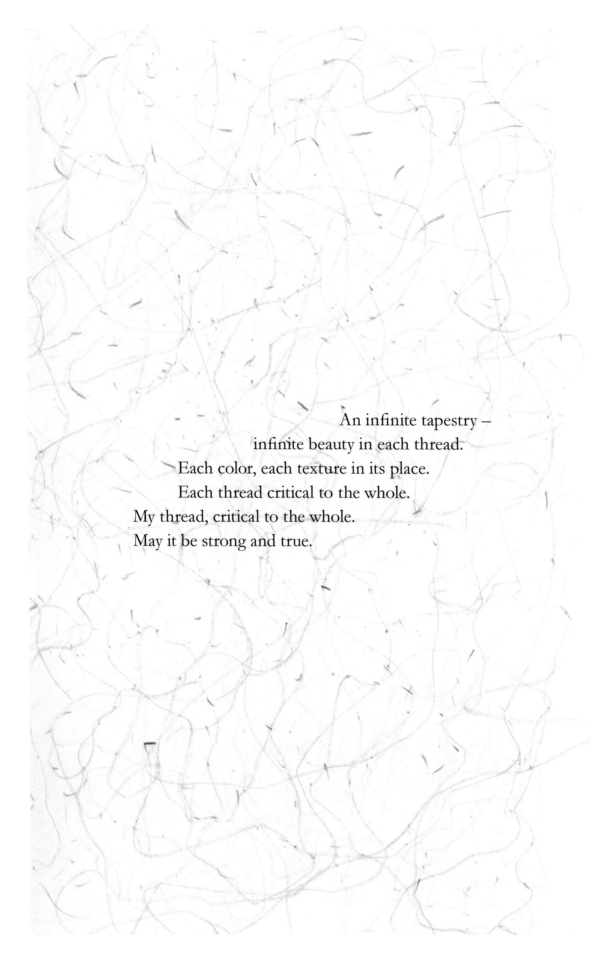

An infinite tapestry –
infinite beauty in each thread.
Each color, each texture in its place.
Each thread critical to the whole.
My thread, critical to the whole.
May it be strong and true.

Mind/time builds a wall of fear.
Fear flows through the generations.
Stones pile high, crush, condense,
block
                    Energy and Love.

Timeless, patient Brave Heart stands firm.
    Beautiful Pure Light breaks through the stones,
                washes them away with tears.
    Timeless healing flows through the generations.
                    Love and Light caress them all.

                Yield control.
                Allow the flow.
                Trust The One.
                No place for fear.
                No place at all!

Say yes to what I'm afraid of.
Yes to dissolving into Spirit.
Yes to losing control.
Yes to losing safety and security.
Yes to exploding into Spirit.
Yes to allowing myself to be seen as imperfect, weak,
                    out of control, vulnerable.

I explode to Spirit.
I dissolve to Spirit.
I live in Spirit, without control,
            safe and secure.

In letting go is peace and joy.
Open to The One, I relax and melt all boundaries,
        wash away all barriers.
I trust, allow, listen, feel – aware only of joy and Love.

Boundless endless Spirit Love –
Mother Mary takes my hand.
Ruth Ann walks beside me all the way.
Daniel stands guard at every step.
My spirit guides surround me, help me clear debris.
Jesus, Archangel Michael, healing angels protect above
                              and below.
Great Spirit enfolds all in Love.
          My part: take Mother Mary's hand, walk the path,
               protected and supported, healed,
                         enfolded in Love.

          Infinite, unbounded, grounded in no-place,
               grounded in Spirit,
                    Beautiful Pure Light of Brave Heart
                              stands ready.

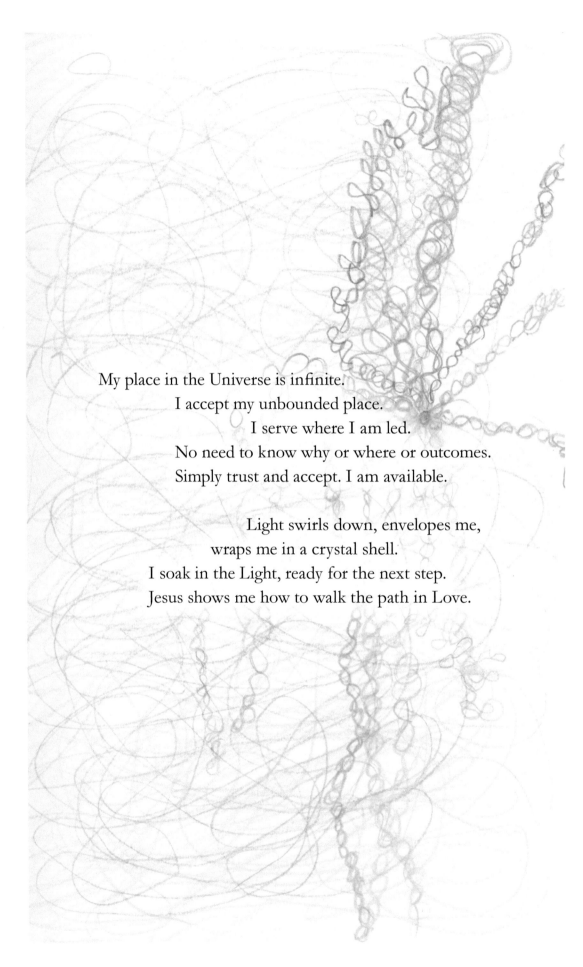

My place in the Universe is infinite.
I accept my unbounded place.
I serve where I am led.
No need to know why or where or outcomes.
Simply trust and accept. I am available.

Light swirls down, envelopes me,
wraps me in a crystal shell.
I soak in the Light, ready for the next step.
Jesus shows me how to walk the path in Love.

Locked-in tears –
body, mind, spirit rigid, inflexible, vulnerable.

My body sinks into a golden cloud, flooded
By golden light.
Fleece absorbs the darkness, draws it out,
Sends it deep into the earth.
Heaven's golden Light floods empty places, caresses,
strengthens.

Freely flowing healing tears –
body, mind, spirit resilient, flexible, strong.
Available to serve.
Heaven's tears flow down, blend with mine.
We wash the Universe.

My tears, heaven's tears. All one.

Healing tears, cleansing tears, wash away
debris, leave openings.
Light and Love fill my heart and
mind and body.
Allow the healing tears to flow.

My truth is Love.
  Love, like water, flows around me, through my cracks.
      Heals me, fills me, overflows, radiating from me.
    Finds cracks, seeps in and heals – revealing only Love.

My love flows with your love, with your love – and yours –
                                          and yours.
  A single trickle, then a river, lake, ocean of Love.
  Evaporates into parched air, rains down on parched earth,
    always loving, always flowing.

My jewels, my treasures – they touch me, always moving,
nudging me along the path.
Steadying me,
nourishing me,
supporting me.

We earth spirits walk along the path connected
      by our common soul through countless generations.
Each raises spirit, strengthens spirit, expands spirit
          in service to The One.
But:
      in each instant, we all are one – no separation
        except in mind-time.

36

Empty boxes in disarray waiting to be filled, waiting
to be used with purpose.

I release the boundaries and blocks.
I release the tears and pain, empty and ready to be filled
with power and strength and joy.
Motivated by the joy of being.
Strength in body, mind and spirit waits.

Bull's strong, feminine energy
connects with the Universe —
sees, hears, knows things others do not know.

I open to the Universe, embrace, melt into Love.
One with Spirit, one with Earth,
Flowing freely, dancing with joy.

I refract the Light to all the Universe.
I embrace all, love all, feel all.
Come dance with me!

The strength to stay frozen

                    or

               the strength to allow melting.

The control to stay frozen

                    or

               the control to yield.

My power is in the yielding, finding the current,

"going with the flow."

 Nothing lost in the melting

               except the illusion.

My love flows to find the cracks where it can enter to

               soothe a troubled spirit.

Love flows back to me, finds my cracks, and enters,

                  soothes my troubled spirit.

Love is the fuel of Being.
Being is the fuel of Love.

I embrace all things.
I am all things.
I am perfection.

Perfection is dull and stagnant.
    My childlike self seeks joy and wonder –
        to run through the grass, splash in the sea,
    Feel the whisper of the breeze, the loving
                warmth of the sun.
    She wants to think and feel all things,
                to share the Love with all,
        to show her cracks and absorb
                the healing Oneness.
    She wants to grow and be all things.

I am deeply loved and deeply blessed.
My only responsibility is to accept the Love and pass it on.
Great Spirit directs me,
    gently nudges me forward into the dark unknown,
        shedding Light along the way.
I move into the darkness, protected by the Love.

Energy seeks free-flow.
Fear, alert, perceives danger, blocks flow.
Energy stagnates, seeks to push through.
Tightens. Seeks a way around.
Fear freezes.

Energy patiently, like water, wears the block away.

I am Brave Heart — always, ever.
    Courageous in the face of challenges throughout the ages.
I move strongly, confidently, forward, deeply knowing
        the peace that lies ahead.
 I reside in Beautiful Pure Light.
        She carries me, courageous and strong.
        She is tenacious, learning to trust her own
                Brave Heart and the Universe.
No worthiness required.
Simply yielding, trusting, being.
She leads us on in faith.

                    Just be, just allow.
                    Accept the gift.
    No struggle, no doing is required.
            Just be, just allow.
    The path is open, waiting.
    Spirit controls the outcome.

My life – a gift I've been given.
      My gift to the Universe –
           walk in faith on the path as I am led.
      Fulfill my life purpose without knowing it.

      My wisdom self – my little child. Listen to her.
          She will lead. She holds the answers.
     I accept the answers.
     I move into the unknown, the Unknowable,
trusting Great Spirit and Beautiful Pure Light
               to lead me on my true path.

My wisdom self – my little child was wounded.
      Now, she's healed and whole –
        free to be in all her glory –
          bright and filled with joy.
      Dancing in her Light, loving all creation.

Jumping into the abyss – not a jump – a slow, cautious
                                               descent
        fighting fear at every step,
        clinging to tenacious faith to keep me on the path.

Oh, to have the faith to take the leap – down to the passageway, through
      to the Light, the Oneness!
     or
   to leap across the gulf straight to the Light,
      leap down into the darkness, tethered and secure.

Ah, my dear, you are all there is.
I am all there is.
The One flows through us without ceasing.
Allow the flow!

Fear of the unknown –
　　Fear of moving forward.
　　Ego wants, needs, demands control.

I feel guilty --
I'm not dong enough.
I must work harder.

But it's not about my work,
It's about my allowing, releasing,
　　yielding to the healing.
I allow. I trust. I yield.

Her love enfolds, surrounds me.
No limits, no conditions – only Love.
Buried in her arms, I melt and flow.

The only Truth:
     Great Spirit is Love, unchanging in
                ceaseless change.
   Endless flow, always returning
     to the One Still Center from which all comes.

I am the center of my web.
You are the center of yours.
Infinite centers, infinite webs,
touching, touching, interweaving
constantly shifting patterns.
Always connected, always connecting.

Intuition, creativity wants, needs, demands the new, the boundless.
Chick spreads her wings, flies straight
into the scary, boundless place
where all is possible,
all is Love.

From life comes death. From death comes life.
Transformation.

Love needs a still place to rest –

                             needs always to move.

   Stillness, flow, stillness, flow, stillness, flow,

   Stillness – eases into motion slowly, faster,

                    slowly, faster, caressing its target.

All is its target.

Nothing is untouched.

Deep within, I am the place of refuge and transformation.

From the place of stillness and decay
	flows life and light – all things new.
From Light and growth, flow nourishment
and purification –
	Back to a place of rest and renewal..
		All moves from stillness.
		All returns to stillness.

I am immersed in Love –

        nothing to do, only to be –

      to allow myself to be led in the direction I must go.

I am wrapped in Love. We all are.

I allow myself to feel the warm, gentle, liquid,

                  breeze of Love surrounding me –

    floating me along the path.

My body is a vessel for a gentle, beautiful soul locked within.
How can I free her?
I can't.
I can allow her to be free.
Fly out, my dear!

Cells release what they've held firm:
fear, self-doubt, anger, fear.
Space now for confidence and joy.
For laughter and joy.

Each little flower, each little leaf in its own place
          pulsing its own color, its own shape,
creating the shape of the whole.
     (with thanks to St. Therese, The Little Flower)

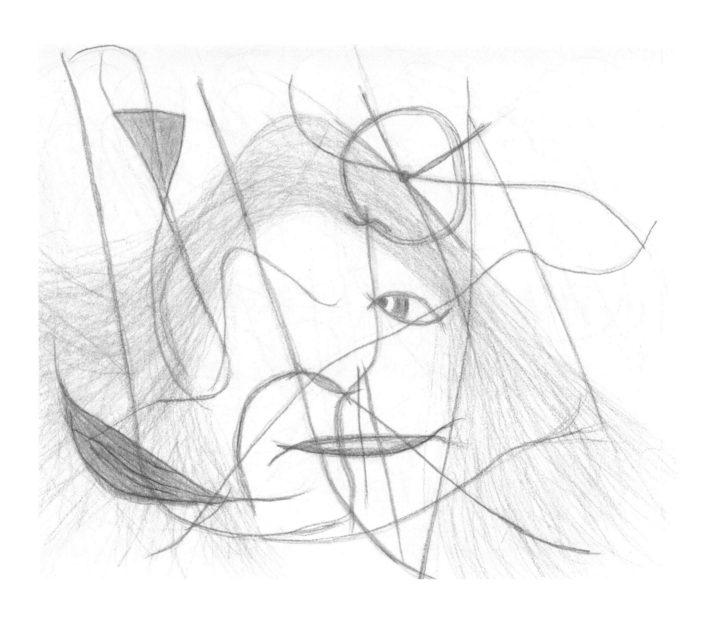

Beautiful Light is a messy one.
     She wants her hands in the paint, to scribble
          and scrawl.
     She wants to run and play and
          spin and swirl,
dancing in her Light.

Flying in the breeze, I find my way home.

I am guided in all I do.

Postscript

Time flows slow like cooling lava, quick like sun-sparks on a waterfall.
Time is transparent, an illusion--
                    dancing, teasing, spinning, weaving
                              free-form out in space.
Time advances--bold, cruel, unrelenting; recedes,
                gossamer-like.
        A touch shatters its fragility.

Time shimmers, melts all together, golden in one piece.
                    Time stops, an instant freezes forever.
                              Past time, present time,
        Dreamtime.

Notes

Beautiful Pure Light = the symbolic meaning of Linda Sue Lucas, my birth name

Brave Heart = my eternal name

Ruth Ann = A spirit guide who has been with me always

Daniel = my guardian angel

"my jewels, my treasures" = The Jewel Tree of Tibet is decorated with pictures or symbols of all of the teachers, guides, and others who have influenced a person's life. Each person can choose to create his or her own tree.

It is said, "The Light comes and floods us all"

I thank all of the people who have supported and helped me and who still do so. Thanks especially to Ken, Joy, Pam, Julie, Sara, Betty Lou, Rachel, Marjorie, and Jessica. You are all represented on my personal Jewel Tree. Your encouragement keeps me on the path.

Printed in the United States
By Bookmasters